This journal belo

IT'S NOT THAT DEEP

The Proper Perception Produces Positivity & Peace.

By: Markisha Baker & Sean Baker

INTRODUCTION

Welcome to the "It's Not That Deep" journal, your path to a positive outlook on life. This journal is intended to lead the reader/participant to a place of mindfulness, positivity, and peace.

The world is a hectic place, and we often get distracted with so many miniscule things. Therefore, this journal paves a path to positive perspectives by giving you the space to reflect on your life.

"It's Not That Deep" offers journal prompts, inspirational quotes, and life scenarios designed to speak to different aspects of our daily lives. It is meant to be uplifting and offer a sense of calm.

Great things come from journaling: reflection, self-awareness, and peace. It helps you discover what empowers and inspire you. If you take the time daily to reflect it can become very therapeutic. We often over-think things, but it we stop and shift focus, we will realize that it's not that deep!

ABOUT THE AUTHORS

Markisha Baker, MBA:

Markisha Baker was born in Long Island, New York. She grew up in Raleigh, North Carolina where she began journaling at an early age. Throughout her formative years, Markisha grew a love for reading and writing. It is where she found solace while growing up in a large family. Her grandmother instilled in her the value of education, and after obtaining a Bachelor's and Master's degree, Markisha began her professional career and continued to journal through. Her love for journaling has been her sounding board, secret keeper, and therapy. When she is not journaling or writing, she enjoys traveling, listening to music, and spending time with family.

Sean A. Baker, M.A., L.C.P.C:

Sean A. Baker was born and raised in S.E. Washington, D.C. He was always a very social person and got along with everybody with whom he came in contact. Sports, mainly football, quickly became his outlet and path to success. With his talent and all conference football award everyone knew he would play college football and be on to the NFL. Turns out one of the coaches on his High School team was also the School Counselor and this Counselor and Coach helped Sean and his family tremendously. This took Sean's focus away from football and motivated him to become a counselor and be that amazing support for someone else like his Coach did for him. Now he is a Licensed Clinical Professional Counselor (LCPC) and practicing in Maryland at Lighthouse Center for Therapy & Play, LLC.

TABLE OF CONTENTS:

Chapter 1: Start Where You Are

Chapter 2: But All My Friends Are Doing It

Chapter 3: Social Media

Chapter 4: Don't Take It Personally

Chapter 5: Critics

Chapter 6: Projection

Chapter 7: It's Okay to Change Your Mind

Chapter 8: Positive Vibes – Mindfulness Techniques

Chapter 9: Consider Alternatives

Chapter 10: Bucket List

CHAPTER 1: START WHERE YOU ARE

Current Mood:

Welcome to the beginning of your journaling journey and starting on the path to peace and positivity. Society today floods us with negativity on a consistent basis and now it is time for us to regain control of our mental health and produce our own positivity and peace in our lives.

Today I feel:

_____
_____
_____
_____
_____
_____
_____
_____
_____
_____
_____
_____
_____
_____
_____
_____

In order to know where you want to go you have to know exactly where you are, so let us check in on your current mood. To do this we will use the **Mood and Feelings Questionnaire** (MFQ) Short Version that was developed by Adrian Angold and Elizabeth J. Costello in 1987.

For each question, please put a check mark in the box that closely describes how you have been feeling or acting for at least the past two weeks.

- ➢ If a sentence was not true about you, check NOT TRUE.
- ➢ If a sentence was only sometimes true, check SOMETIMES.
- ➢ If a sentence was true about you most of the time, check TRUE.

Score your MFQ as follows:

- ➢ NOT TRUE = 0
- ➢ SOMETIMES = 1
- ➢ TRUE = 2

Please use a check mark for each statement.	NOT TRUE	SOME TIMES	TRUE
1. I felt miserable or unhappy.			
2. I didn't enjoy anything at all.			
3. I felt so tired I just sat around & did nothing.			
4. I was very restless.			
5. I felt I was no good anymore.			
6. I cried a lot.			
7. I found it hard to think properly or concentrate.			
8. I hated myself.			
9. I was a bad person.			
10. I felt lonely.			
11. I thought nobody really loved me.			
12. I thought I could never be as good as other people.			
13. I did everything wrong.			

Child MFQ (ages: 6-18)

Please use a check mark for each statement.	NOT TRUE	SOME TIMES	TRUE
1. I felt miserable or unhappy.			
2. I didn't enjoy anything at all.			
3. I felt so tired I just sat around & did nothing.			
4. I was very restless.			
5. I felt I was no good anymore.			
6. I cried a lot.			
7. I found it hard to think properly or concentrate.			
8. I hated myself.			
9. I was a bad person.			
10. I felt lonely.			
11. I thought nobody really loved me.			
12. I thought I could never be as good as other kids.			
13. I did everything wrong.			

Once you finish, add up your score.

If you scored 12 or higher this may indicate the presence of depression and we strongly encourage you to find and begin seeing a Licensed Mental Health Professional (MHP).

Use the space below to list your MHP research

MHP #1	
Business Name:	
MHP Name:	
Address:	
Phone Number:	
Website:	
Session Cost:	
Insurance Accepted:	

MHP #2	
Business Name:	
MHP Name:	
Address:	
Phone Number:	
Website:	
Session Cost:	
Insurance Accepted:	

"Start where you are. Use what you have. Do what you can." – Arthur Ashe

MHP #3	
Business Name:	
MHP Name:	
Address:	
Phone Number:	
Website:	
Session Cost:	
Insurance Accepted:	

MHP #4	
Business Name:	
MHP Name:	
Address:	
Phone Number:	
Website:	
Session Cost:	
Insurance Accepted:	

Tips for finding a therapist:
- Consult your provider directory
- Ask someone you trust
- Use an online database
- Explore local resources
- Reach out to organizations that address your areas of concern
- Try online therapy apps

Courtesy of: www.healthline.com

GOALS:
Now that you have completed this Questionnaire, we would like to give you a chance to reflect on your results and, also come up with steps you would like to take to improve upon your current mood and set self-care goals for yourself.

_____
_____
_____
_____
_____

Now we would like for you to take your goals and make them even better by turning them into **SMART goals.**

S = Specific: What do you want to accomplish? Who needs to be included? When do you want to do this? Why is this a goal?

M = Measurable: How can you measure progress and know if you've successfully met your goal?

A = Achievable: Do you have the skills required to achieve the goal? If not, can you obtain them? What is the motivation for this goal? Is the amount of effort required on par with what the goal will achieve?

R = Relevant: Why am I setting this goal now? Is it aligned with my overall objectives?

T = Time: What's the deadline and is this deadline realistic?

Initial Goal: Write the goal(s) you have in mind

_____
_____
_____
_____
_____
_____
_____
_____

> "Setting goals is the first step in turning the invisible into the visible." – Tony Robbins

Now that you have answered these questions, review what you have written and write your new SMART Goal Statement based on what your answers above have revealed.

At this point you're probably thinking, this SMART goal will take me forever to complete. When goals take a long time to accomplish the success rate typically goes down. This is due to the fact that majority of people love instant gratification. So, in order to set yourself up for success set some short-term goals that will help you reach your SMART goal. SMART goals have a lot of steps and usually they take time to reach so these are typically long-term goals. It is very important to have short term and long-term goals to keep yourself motivated and to increase the chances your goal(s) being achieved.

SHORT TERM GOALS	LONG TERM GOAL

While thinking and making your SMART goals you probably realized that your personal and career goals have overlapped a bit or maybe even overlapped a lot. You want to separate those to help you set clear boundaries between your personal and professional life. Often times we don't have a healthy work life balance and we want to definitely make sure to end that bad habit. A healthy work life balance leads to better quality of life, which leads to positivity and peace.

PERSONAL GOALS	PROFESSIONAL GOALS

Take a breather to reflect:

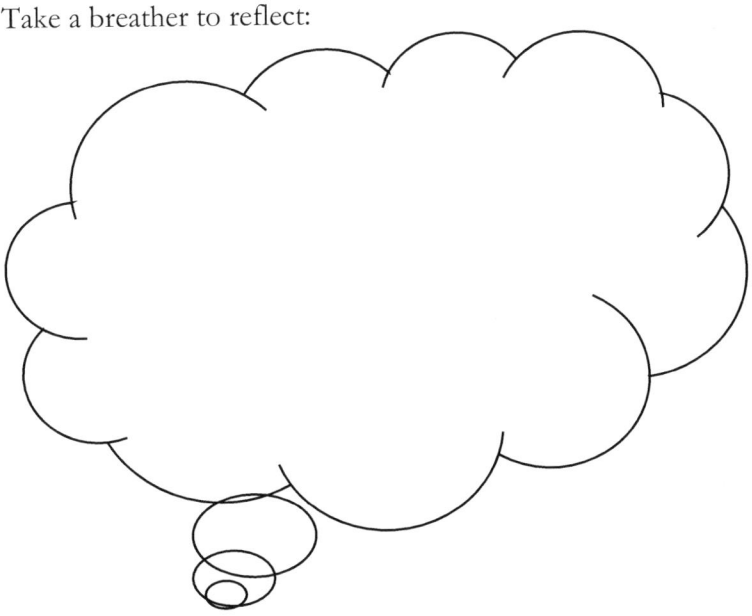

Obstacles:

Life will always find a way to throw obstacles in your path. A mentally healthy person will be able to navigate life's obstacles will little to no disruption in their daily living. If something is having a consistent negative impact on your daily living skills, then that is a key indicator of a decline in a person's mental health.

If you begin to notice you are having trouble getting out of bed, loss of interest in things that normally interest you, not keeping up with personal hygiene, isolating yourself from others, etc. These are just a few things to be aware of because they all can be indicators of depression. When a person feels depressed, it is extremely difficult to foster positivity and peace, but it is not impossible. You must be very intentional about doing things that impact your mood in a positive way and continue doing those things in order to push through life's obstacles.

Sometimes the obstacles we face trigger various emotions for us. We also must remember that no emotion is negative, it's how we express those emotions that can make the experience negative. Lashing out at our loved ones is a prime example of how having emotions can negatively impact us and those around us. Later on in this journal we will cover defense mechanism. Lashing out can be categorized as a common defense mechanism known as Displacement.

At this time, we would like for you to think about any obstacles you are currently dealing with and any obstacles you think may hinder you from reaching your goal(s). We also want you to think of realistic ways you can overcome these obstacles.

> "The greater the obstacle, the more glory in overcoming it." - Moliere

Here are some obstacles that can get in the way of goals:

- ➢ Excuses
- ➢ Perfectionism
- ➢ Procrastination
- ➢ Taking big steps
- ➢ Focusing on the end result
- ➢ Distractions
- ➢ Expectations
- ➢ Lack of consistency

Relationships:

It is very important to pay attention to the company you keep when trying to protect your peace and foster positivity. Negativity is contagious, but the good news is positivity is too. When you think about your family, friends, romantic partners, etc. be sure to consider how their energy impacts you. Sometimes we must realize that even though we love somebody they may not always be good for us.

Every healthy relationship needs healthy boundaries, and those boundaries should be communicated. Prime example when a family is too enmeshed it can create friction. It also can make you take on the negative beliefs of others and prevent you from even attempting your goal. The last thing we want to do is allow another person's negative opinion stop us from accomplishing our goals.

In order to combat that negative energy some people benefit from writing down positive affirmations or writing down positive things/experiences that they have had. We like to call is a positivity bank. It is important to make regular deposits into your positivity bank so that when you are having a bad day or a rough obstacle has gotten in your way, you can make a withdrawal from your positivity bank.

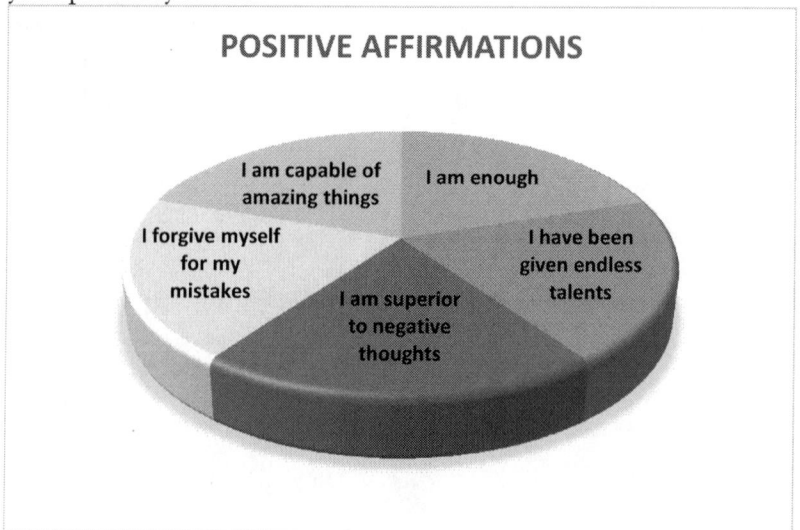

Positivity Bank
Make your deposits here:

This is just one example of how to be intentional about creating positivity in your life and finding peace. You can also get creative with your positivity bank. It could be a small box that closes or locks, a folder, or even a piggy bank that you can open/uncork on the bottom. When you have free time, and you are writing in this journal make sure you have some post it notes or small pieces of paper so that you can jot down positive things and deposit them into your bank. When time get hard it is helpful to reflect on positive things rather than get fixated on the negative things. Focusing on negativity can also hinder your ability to problem solve and can make you less resilient when faced with adversity.

> "Success is to be measured not so much by the position that one has reached in life as by the obstacles which he has overcome while trying to succeed." – Booker T. Washington

Woosah! Take a breather!

CHAPTER 2: BUT ALL MY FRIENDS ARE DOING IT

Comparisons:

It can be easy to look at your peers/friends and make decisions on how your life should be or look. Life has taught us that we should be held to some level of scrutiny. When we are in grade school, we should be reading or learning at the same level as our peers. When we are in college, we have four years to earn a degree, and when we go to work, we are evaluated on the work that we do. So, it can be extremely difficult not to think that your/our lives should be comparable to our peers. However, we are here to tell you that "It's not that deep!"

There are benefits to living your life as you want.

Here are some amazing things that happen when you stop comparing your life to others:

- You gain self-worth
- You embrace your individuality
- You gain self-acceptance
- You have more gratitude
- You learn who you are

> "When you know yourself, you are empowered. When you accept yourself you ae invincible!" – Tina Lifford

Think about your goals, what you are doing, and where you are headed. Take a moment to reflect and think if these things are because you genuinely want them or if you are doing them because all your friends are doing it.

Ponder here:

_____
_____
_____
_____
_____
_____
_____
_____
_____
_____
_____
_____
_____
_____

> "Comparison is an act of violence against self" - Iyanla Vanzant

Comparison Chart:

Scenario	Positive Spin
All of my friends have purchased a home and I am still living in my parents basement.	I am building a nest egg and improving my credit, so that I can buy the house that I want and not just the one that I can afford at the moment.
All of my friends are married and starting a family, and I am still dating.	I am free to travel, meet new people, and explore the world whenever I want.
I was fired from my job.	This is an opportunity to reavalute, learn a new skill, and decide what I really want to do with my life.
My friends make way more money than me.	I am doing what I love to do.
All of my friends are going to college and I don't want to.	I will take this time to learn a skill/trade and explore other options for my life.

Things you don't need to justify:

- Who you love or why you love them
- Changing your career or direction in life
- What you choose to prioritize
- When or how often you take breaks
- Ending a toxic friendship/relationship
- The way you spend your free time

Create your own timetable for your life:

No one can live your life but you! So, why would you live according to others timeline. It can be difficult but don't let others' expectations determine how you live your life.

Below are some questions that can be triggering:
- When are you going to have kids?
- When are you getting married?
- Don't you think it's time to settle down?
- Why are you still pursuing that dream?
- Why are you still renting?

These aforementioned questions are a result of someone else's perception and the timeline that they have designed for themselves. Try not to let these questions bother you. Remember, "It's not that deep!"

Now, think about the things that you want to do in your lifetime. Remember them when you begin to second-guess the things that you are doing in your life.

> "Tis better to live your own life imperfectly, than to imitate someone else's perfectly." - Elizabeth Gilbert

Use this space to write down the things that you wish to accomplish:

_____
_____
_____
_____
_____
_____
_____
_____
_____
_____
_____
_____
_____
_____
_____

After you know what you want to accomplish, it will be much easier to start a plan. Also, keep in mind that it is perfectly fine if the plans change.

> "You can't go back and change the beginning but, you can start where you are and change the ending." - Unknown

It's okay to start over:

Starting over is not easy, but if something is no longer serving you, it is best to start over instead of living a life you no longer want. Try not to look at starting over as failure. In fact, it is very much the opposite! It take's knowledge, strength, and courage to start over.

Questions to ask yourself:
- ➢ Am I happy with my life and the direction it is going?
- ➢ Do I feel stuck?
- ➢ Am I fulfilled with the work that I do?
- ➢ Is there something that I have always wanted to try?

Ponder here:

How to start over when you feel stuck:
www.thriveglobal.com

1. Start with cleaning up the space you live in.
2. Make peace with reality and work with, not against it.
3. Reflect on what and where you went wrong.
4. Revisit your goals and values.
5. Decide what you want to do next.
6. Work up the courage to do it.
7. Identify the obstacles standing in your way.
8. Design a plan to eliminate these obstacles.
9. Overcome your fear of being wrong.
10. Get a mentor.

Revisit your goals:

_____
_____
_____
_____
_____
_____
_____
_____
_____

> "Don't let your fear of what could happen make nothing happen." - Unknown

Identify obstacles:
_____
_____
_____
_____
_____
_____
_____
_____

Plan to eliminate obstacles:
_____
_____
_____
_____
_____
_____
_____
_____

Get a mentor

Tips:

- ➢ Go over your goals
- ➢ Ask about your workplace mentorship program
- ➢ Search online
- ➢ Attend events related to your interests
- ➢ Use a professional mentor service

Use this space to list potential mentors:

_____
_____
_____
_____
_____
_____
_____
_____
_____

"A mentor is someone who allows you to see the hope inside yourself." – Oprah Winfrey

Check your ego:

It is important to not let your ego get in the way of reaching your Dreams.

Ego says:

- ➢ I'm too old to start over
- ➢ I will be embarrassed
- ➢ I will look weak if I ask for help

So, check your ego and know that "It's not that deep!"

Take a moment to reflect and think about times when you let your ego get in the way. Write them down so that you won't repeat it.

_____
_____
_____
_____
_____
_____
_____
_____
_____
_____
_____
_____
_____

When thinking about your ego also be sure to remember the human brain is really powerful, so use that power to motive yourself instead of talking yourself out of opportunities. As human we all have needs that need to be met, but according to Abraham Maslow those needs go way beyond food and water. Maslow's Hierarchy of Needs can be directly correlated with Sigmund Freud's psychoanalytic theory of the Id, Ego, and Super Ego.

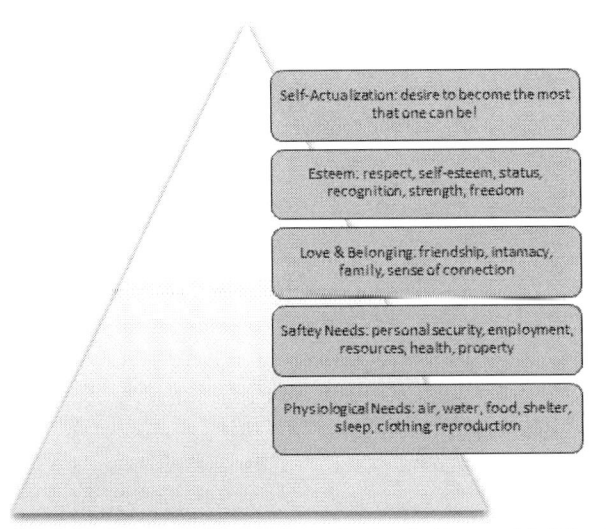

Self-Actualization: desire to become the most that one can be!

Esteem: respect, self-esteem, status, recognition, strength, freedom

Love & Belonging: friendship, intimacy, family, sense of connection

Saftey Needs: personal security, employment, resources, health, property

Physiological Needs: air, water, food, shelter, sleep, clothing, reproduction

Above is Maslow's Hierarchy of Needs Pyramid. The bottom shows us our basic human needs and as we meet those needs our brain takes us up to higher more complex levels of needs. These needs fuel us and if we pay attention to these needs, we can make it to Self-Actualization, at the top of the pyramid, which is where majority of people want to be. Now knowing this piece of information, you can imagine if a person does not meet the needs of a level that person would essentially be "stuck" there.

This is where Freud's psychoanalytic theory of the Id, Ego, and Superego come in. All too often we let pride, embarrassment, and what others think motivate us to do what we really don't want to do. In doing that we neglect our needs and begin to fulfill the needs of others, which can quickly lead to everyone's happiness except yours. Start listening to, what we like to call, your three inner voices (Id, Ego, and Superego).

Id	Ego	Superego
- Impusive - Fulfills Deep Desires - Taps into our unconcious - Pleasure Principle	- Realistic - Problem Solving - Helps us aviod negative or unwanted consequences - Compromising between your Id and Supergo.	- Based in good morals and values - Typically motivates us to strive for perfection - Attempts to keep the Id's impulses under control

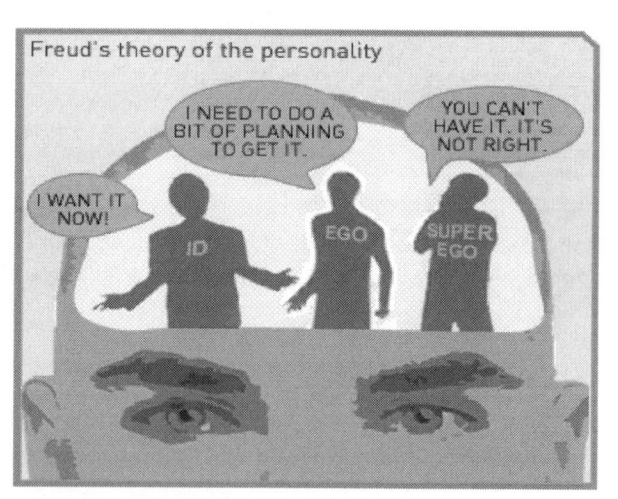

Freud's theory of the personality

I WANT IT NOW!
ID

I NEED TO DO A BIT OF PLANNING TO GET IT.
EGO

YOU CAN'T HAVE IT. IT'S NOT RIGHT.
SUPER EGO

This Photo by Unknown Author is licensed under CC BY-NC-ND

Your Inner Wisdom	Your Ego
Feels calm and quiet	Is loud and wants to shut out others opinions
Is based in love	Is based in fear or some other negative emotion
Is concerned about the greater good	Is concerned with itself
Feels as peace	Feels angry, tense, hyper, jealous
Is not emotionally invested in the outcomes	Feels threathened if it doesn't get its way
Is consistent	It changes based on your mood
Is patient	Is not patient
Needs no excuses	Has plenty of excuses and justifications
You feel you can trust it	Is full of rationalizations & explanations to try to make it feel right
You sense the voice is coming from your core	You sense the voice is coming from your head

www.christinebradstreet.com

Woosah! Take a breather

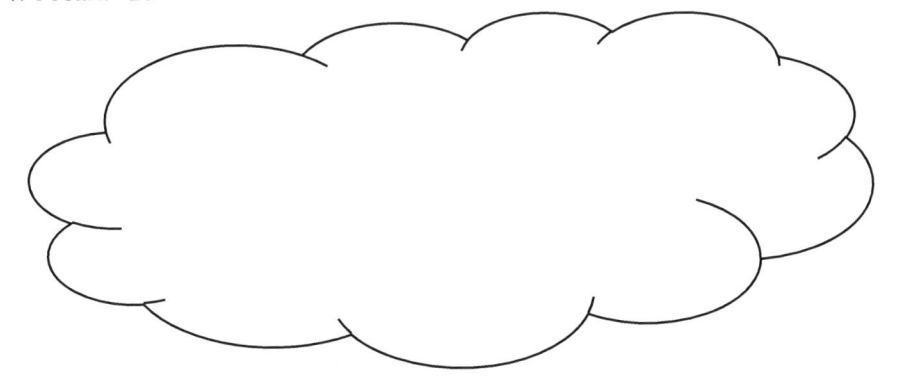

CHAPTER 3: SOCIAL MEDIA

Social media allows people to create and share content, socialize, and network. While the intentions for social media may be positive, it has several influences on our lives. It has become an intricate part of most people's lives. However, we often give social media more credit than it deserves when it comes to the influence that it has on our lives.

PROS OF SOCIAL MEDIA:
- Allows you to keep in touch with people
- Promotes social change
- Speeds up communication
- Supports personal growth
- Promote businesses
- Influences you to live a healthy life
- Enables you to become an inspiration

CONS OF SOCIAL MEDIA:
- Decreases face-to-face communication
- Lacks emotional connections
- Gives license to be hurtful
- Can spread false information
- Facilitates laziness
- Causes distractions
- Can create a skewed self-image

> "Everything you post on social media impacts your personal brand. How do you want to be remembered?" – Lisa Horn

What do you think your personal brand has become on social media:

_____
_____
_____
_____
_____
_____
_____
_____
_____

What do you like about your social media page:

_____
_____
_____
_____
_____
_____
_____
_____
_____

What would you like to change about your social media page:

_____
_____
_____
_____
_____
_____
_____
_____

Don't believe the hype:

Social media is a highlight reel and people post what they want you to see. So, try not to fall in the trap of comparing your life to others based on their posts. Consider the reasons why people post what they post. They could be looking for praise or a "pick-me-up." They could be looking for a distraction from the harsh realities of their true life, or they could simply be liars.

Consider these scenarios and alternatives:

What they post	What they don't post
My friend was promoted at work and received a sizeable pay increase.	They work environment is hostile and feel stuck.
My friend's child was accepted to 5 colleges.	We have no idea how to cover the expenses.
My friend's spouse just bought them a brand new Porsche.	This is an apology gift because the spouse is cheating.
My friend is on vacation in a tropical island.	The trip maxed out their creidt card and they really can't afford the trip.

Keep in mind that social media posts are controlled. It should not be a tool by which to measure our lives. Remember, it's not that deep.

> "Just because it is not on Social Media, doesn't mean it's not happening."

Think before you post personal information on social media. People can create narratives about your life simply by looking at the pictures that you post.

Hit That Unfollow button:

It is important that we protect our peace. If someone's page is impacting you in a negative way, unfollowing them can be beneficial. Someone's page should not control your emotions. The people, thoughts, and ideas that you allow into your social space, can make a significant impact to your overall wellbeing. Remember, it costs you nothing to hit unfollow.

Here are a few reasons to unfollow:
- You find yourself disagreeing with their beliefs
- They are always in some drama
- They are too negative
- Their posts make you angry
- They post a lot of misleading information
- BECAUSE YOU WANT TO!

Think about times when you allowed social media to interrupt your peace:

_____
_____
_____
_____
_____
_____
_____
_____

> "Don't let the behavior of others destroy your inner peace." – Dalai Lama

Woosah! Take a breather

CHAPTER 4: DON'T TAKE IT PERSONALLY

Nothing Others Do is Because of You:

Often times we feel that the actions of others are our fault, and we begin to fall into the trap of internalizing. Instead of evaluating a situation for what it is we sometimes blame ourselves even if we had little to no control over the outcome. A common example would be a person blaming themselves for their romantic partner cheating on them. Now do we all have flaws? Yes, but those flaws do not make a person cheat on you, NO. We all have to ability as humans to make decisions based on what needs/wants we wish to fulfill. Like we spoke about in the previous chapter, we have a part of our brain that drives and motivates us to act impulsively to fulfill our wants and deep desires (Id). No matter how right or wrong those desires might be the "Id" part of our brain gives us the green light.

Ponder That:

Now that we know how the brain plays a part in motivating us hopefully that gives you the permission to stop blaming yourself for the actions of others. In order to truly free yourself from the negativity and foster positivity and peace in your life you must be able to accurately evaluate situations and accept them. Sometimes we overanalyze things and as a result we've created things and scenarios that don't even exist and stress ourselves out. If we take the time to look at the facts and accept them, we can better identify our emotions and act accordingly.

Being able to experience all emotions is healthy and we should not want to go through life feeling one emotion all the time or feeling numb. Society has placed a somewhat negative connotation on "emotional" people but in all actuality it's not the emotion that's negative. It is what we do with our emotions and how we behave when experiencing those various emotions that can be a positive experience or a negative one. This is why realizing that the actions of others are NOT your fault is very important. If we make everything about us and make everything our fault, we aren't fostering positivity, we're fostering the exact opposite.

> "What other people think about me is none of my business." - Unknown

Please take this time to recall a time when you blamed yourself for the actions of others:

_____
_____
_____
_____
_____
_____
_____
_____

Things to remember:
- I cannot control others
- I can only be responsible for MY actions
- Others should take responsibility for their actions instead of me taking responsibility for their actions
- Less overthinking = Less Stress
- Others only have power/control over us if we allow it

Cognitive Reframing:

Cognitive Reframing is a psychological technique that helps a person identify a situation and then alter the way that person views that particular situation in order to help them. For example, a person lost their job due to the pandemic and they are feeling like they have hit rock bottom. Cognitive reframing would help that person identify exactly how they feel about that situation and help them find ways to make this seemingly negative situation look more like an opportunity to land that dream job or start that small business. To sum up Cognitive Reframing would be to say, "when life gives you lemons make lemonade!"

We all have the power to be mentally strong and healthy already within us, we just have to do the work to tap into that strength. Like they say, "if you don't use it, you lose it." That phrase definitely applies to us working our mental muscles and being mentally healthy. If we allow stressful and negative situations to linger in our brains and we do nothing to try to shift our mindset, then we set ourselves up to be depressed and stuck in the very place we don't want to be in.

If you ever find yourself in a dark place and you feel stuck or feel depressed it does not hurt to ask for help. It takes a strong person to ask for help because that's the sign of a person trying to make a change for the better. We all know what doing the same thing and expecting new results gets us, insanity. So, identify and utilize your support system. If you feel that you need more then add a licensed mental health professional to your support system. They are the professionals so allow them to assist you with cognitive reframing. Every battle is not meant for you to fight alone.

> "People begin to become successful the minute they decide to be." – Harvey Mackay

Great websites to help you find a licensed mental health professional in your area:

- www.psychologytoday.com
- https://screening.mhanational.org/content/how-do-i-find-therapist/
- https://www.apa.org/ptsd-guideline/patients-and-families/finding-good-therapist

_____
_____
_____
_____
_____
_____
_____
_____
_____
_____
_____
_____

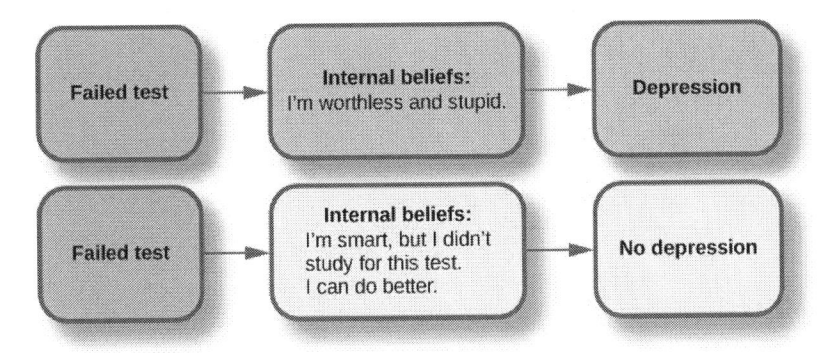

| Failed test | → | Internal beliefs: I'm worthless and stupid. | → | Depression |
| Failed test | → | Internal beliefs: I'm smart, but I didn't study for this test. I can do better. | → | No depression |

This Photo by Unknown Author is licensed under **CC BY**

Cognitive reframing can be powerful!

Worry About What You Can Control:

We often become very fixated on the things that are beyond our control. This is typically because we feel that people should do things a certain way. We must be careful with thinking about what people "should" do because who are we to say what others "should" be doing with their lives. When we think in terms of what others should be doing, we are imposing our values and worldview onto them and that is not fair to either of us. Trying to impose our values and worldview onto others only creates more stress in our lives. It creates stress because we begin to worry about things that are beyond our control. Worrying also stems from us thinking about the future, which is also something we have no control over.

When trying to find peace in your world you have to be where your feet are! I know your read that and went what in the world does that mean? It means try to live in the present moment. We live in a world where social media, television, and so many other distractions take us away from enjoying our present moments. When we aren't living in the moment, we are most likely worrying about things we probably cannot control and adding to our stress level instead of minimizing it.

One way to manage our stress and focus on the things we can control would be to utilize some Mindfulness techniques.

Check out this website for some amazing Mindfulness Strategies to get started.
https://www.mindful.org/take-a-mindful-moment-5-simple-practices-for-daily-life/

Use this space to write down some of the Mindfulness strategies you will utilize to help you remember to control only what you can control and to relieve stress:

_____
_____
_____
_____
_____
_____
_____
_____
_____
_____
_____
_____

> "There are two kinds of worries—those you can do something about and those you can't. Don't spend any time on the latter." – Duke Ellington

Obligations vs. Choices:

We all know the difference between obligations and choices, but the question is do we put things in its proper category? If you don't put things in the proper category, it's no need to worry, we are all human and we all have been guilty of this at some point in our lives. Sometimes we even blur the lines between the two categories, and we feel lost or out of control of our lives. Now is the time to recognize the mistakes and begin to make a change for the better!

OBLIGATIONS	CHOICES
Taking care of children	Maintaining toxic relationships
Going to work	Going to the office happy hour event
Paying bills on time	Impulse buying online

Sometimes we feel obligated to make the choice that society/others want us to make and that is not the way to go. We must remember that doing what is best for you is NOT selfish! Just because we get an invite to the office happy hour doesn't mean we have to go. Just because your family member is rude and toxic doesn't mean you have to talk to them on the regular or hold conversations at the family functions.

People must start giving themselves permission to please themselves and stop making the choice to do things that they aren't necessarily obligated to do. It's ok to miss an office event if you want to be home relaxing on your couch and saving money. It's ok to be cordial to a toxic family member and love them but from a distance. It's ok to make the choice to do what's best for your and to make pleasing yourself your number one obligation.

Take some time to list out some of your obligations and some of your choices and evaluate them to see if you have them in what YOU feel is the proper category.

OBLIGATIONS	CHOICES

Woosah! Take a breather

CHAPTER 5: CRITICS

The difference between constructive criticism and hate:

Most of you are probably familiar with both of these terms but what you may not be familiar with is that some people feel like these terms are interchangeable. WRONG! Sometimes people feel that what they give others is constructive criticism but in fact they are throwing so much hate. What sets these terms apart is the delivery and the intent behind the words. If the delivery is positive and the intent is to help someone be the best they can be, then it's most likely constructive criticism. If the delivery is rude and was said just to belittle someone then it is probably hate.

When giving legitimate constructive criticism we must consider how the other person will receive what we are going to say and phrase it in a way that is tactful. Also, it is helpful to think about how you would want the news delivered to you and treat the person you are giving the criticism to with the same respect. A good technique to use is one you often hear in cooperate America and in management roles, the sandwich method. This method suggests that you start off your constrictive criticism with a positive statement, next ease into the area that needs to be improved upon, then end with an encouraging statement or identify a strength of the person who you are speaking to.

Now, you are probably thinking to yourself, "I wonder if I give constructive criticism or, have I been hating on others (intentionally or unintentionally)?" In addition to that thought you probably recalled some of the times you found yourself in a situation where you felt someone was hating on you or a supervisor gave you some good constructive criticism during an annual review/evaluation.

Take this time to write down a time when you hated on someone and how that experience made you feel?

Don't listen to your inner critic:

Now that we have gotten that negative past experience off our chest let's take this time to shift our energy towards the positive side. Think of all the things in your life you have accomplished no matter how big or how small. Don't worry sometimes this takes a while to really think about all the victories you've had in your life. Partly because once you start to include those small victories, they begin to add up quickly but also because our brains are basically conditioned to fixate on negative things. The society we live in unfortunately thrives on drama and conflict. Social media and reality TV are prime examples of that. With that being said we have to be mindful of how much time, attention, and energy we give to negativity. Instead of focusing on that negativity that we are used to, we must go out of our way and make a conscious effort every day to focus on positivity and choosing peace!

When it comes to choosing positivity and peace, we must be at peace with ourselves! We all fight inner battles and can be our own worst critic. Please keep in mind that there are plenty of people out there who already are negatively criticizing you, don't become one of them. It's ok to give yourself a sandwich technique pep talk occasionally. We all have flaws, but we also have the power to change our perspective and look at our flaws as areas for growth. If we look at flaws as areas for growth, then we can find ways to motivate ourselves to be the best that we can be instead of just being complacent. Shifting our mindset to be consistently positive is not an easy task but it is possible with the right amount of effort and dedication.

Once you are motivated to shut down your inner critic and live your best life being the best version of yourself you will probably feel a little uncomfortable or you'll find that life will begin to throw some curveballs at you. Stay strong, stay focused, and remember growth can't happen if we live in our comfort zone.

If you feel there are any barriers that keep you from living your best life and being the best version of yourself, write them down here:

"Be mindful of your self-talk. It's a conversation with the universe." - David James Lees

"It's not what we say out loud that really determines our lives. It's what we whisper to ourselves that has the most power." - Unknown

S-0-S
Negative Self-Talk Stopping Technique

S-top: Mentally tell yourself "stop!" to give you the opportunity to address the thought and interrupt the cycle

O-bserve: Observe what you are saying to yourself and how it is making you feel.

S-hift: Shift your cognitive, emotional, or behavioral response by using positive coping skills and techniques.

Now that you have taken the time to account for the possible barriers, it is time to think of ways to overcome those barriers and if you cannot do it on your own who can support you?

Possible barriers	Who can help me overcome those barriers

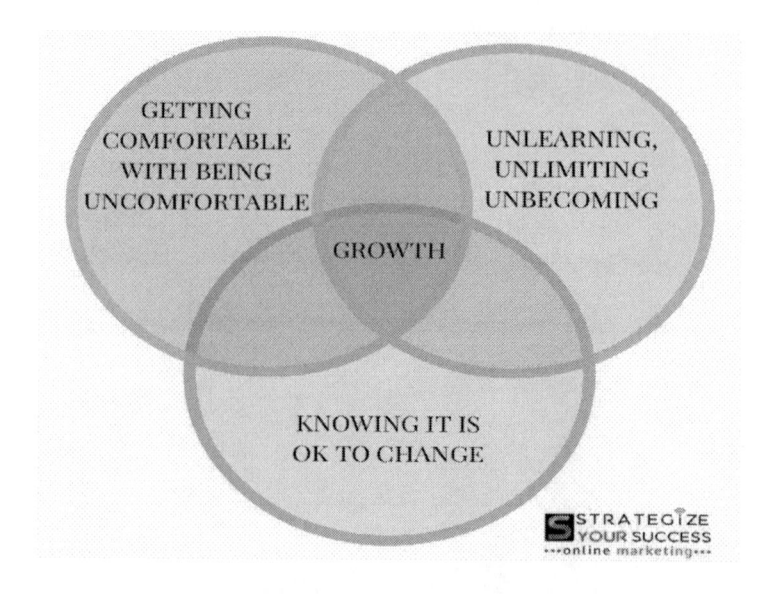

GETTING COMFORTABLE WITH BEING UNCOMFORTABLE

UNLEARNING, UNLIMITING UNBECOMING

GROWTH

KNOWING IT IS OK TO CHANGE

STRATEGIZE YOUR SUCCESS
···online marketing···

Flip it – Criticism can be a positive thing:

Criticism in fact doesn't always have to be seen as a negative thing. As we stated earlier it can be looked at as an area for growth or even an opportunity for improvement. Although people don't always deliver the criticism properly it is up to us to protect our peace and take from it what we need to better ourselves. As Michelle Obama always says, "When they go low, we go high!" It can be very difficult to do this, but I can assure you that you'll be glad you took the high road. Often times the very adversity we hate dealing with is the exact thing we need to push us to our full potential. We sometimes are so caught up in the negative aspect of it all that we lose sight of the wonderful things we can gain by facing this adversity head on.

A prime example would be when a person feels they are in the wrong profession, and they want to switch careers and try to pursue their passion. This person has become comfortable with the average pay and job security so there isn't much desire to switch careers. Then a new supervisor gets hired and they turn out to be a micromanager and gives you a horrible annual review after only working with you for a few months. This person who was complacent with the job that was not their passion was just faced with heavy criticism and can use this very uncomfortable situation as motivation to live in their passion and finally find a sense of peace. Always try to use any criticism that you are given to your advantage, you never know where it might take you!

> "If you don't like something, change it. If you can't change it, change your attitude." – Maya Angelou

Woosah! Take a breather

CHAPTER 6: PROJECTION

What is projection?

In psychology, projection refers to placing your own negative traits or unwanted emotions onto others. It is a defense mechanism in which the ego defends itself against unconscious impulses or qualities by denying their existence in themselves and attributing them to others.

Projection Examples:

> - A cheating spouse who suspects their partner of being unfaithful
> - A friend who has a hostile nature might attribute their hostility to their friend and say they have an anger management problem
> - You may have a strong dislike for someone, you might instead believe that they do not like you.
> - You failed at something, and you convince your friend that they can't do it either and talk them out of it

Use the space below to think about times where you have projected your insecurities onto others (intentionally or unintentionally):

_____
_____
_____
_____
_____
_____
_____
_____

Use the space below to think about times where others have projected their insecurities onto you:

_____
_____
_____
_____
_____
_____
_____
_____

Defense Mechanism

Projection is a form of defense in which unwanted feelings are placed onto others. Defense mechanisms are thought to safeguard the mind against feelings and thoughts that are too difficult for the conscious mind to cope with.

> "My Uncle told me that I would never sell a million records, but I sold a million records like a million times. I know he didn't mean any malice, but he was just projecting, putting his fears on me. He couldn't even see it."
>
> - Shawn 'Jay-Z' Carter

Common Defense Mechanisms:

- ➤ **Rationalization** - involves explaining an unacceptable behavior or feeling in a rational or logical manner, avoiding the true reasons for the behavior
    - o Example: a person who is turned down for a date might rationalize the situation by saying they were not attracted to the other person anyway.
- ➤ **Displacement** – taking out your frustration, feelings and impulses on people or things that are less threatening
    - o Example: Having a bad day at work, then coming home and taking out your frustration on your family or friends.
- ➤ **Repression** - acts to keep information out of conscious awareness. However, the memories don't disappear, they influence behavior.
    - o Example: a person who suffered abuse as a child may later have difficulty forming relationships.
- ➤ **Denial** – protect the individual from things with which they. cannot cope. It's an outright refusal to admit that something is occurring or has occurred
    - o Example: A person struggling with alcohol refusing to admit that they have a problem.
- ➤ **Sublimation** - allows us to act out unacceptable impulses by converting these behaviors into a more acceptable form.
    - o Example: a person experiencing extreme anger might take up martial arts as a means of venting frustration.
- ➤ **Reaction Formation** – when people express the opposite of their true feelings, sometimes to an exaggerated extent
    - o Example: A person would act extremely friendly to someone, but they really despise that person

We have all experienced these examples. It doesn't mean that we are "bad" in any way, it just makes us human. However, now that we know, we can think about our experiences and be better going forward.

On the next pages, take a moment to reflect on your own defense mechanisms.

Rationalization:

Displacement:

Repression:

Denial:

Sublimation:

Reaction Formation:

Don't Let Others Tell You What You Can't Do.

Now that we have learned about projection, we know that when someone tells us that we cannot do something, it may be a form of projection. It is okay to consider someone's advice and experiences, however, try not to let it deter you from doing what you want to do.

We all have our own fears, and we must not let them get in the way of reaching our goals.

Think about the times when you have let someone discourage your from doing what you wanted to do – even those closest to you:

_____
_____
_____
_____
_____
_____
_____
_____
_____
_____
_____
_____
_____

You are Your Own Expert.

We are all unique and therefore our experiences will be too. Remember, you are the master of your destiny. So instead of thinking "I did not apply for a job because someone talked me out of it." We must instead think, "I did not apply for a job because I allowed someone to talk me out of it."

No one can live your life for you therefore, you are the expert of your life. You get to decide what is best for you. You get to make your own goals. You get to travel your own path.

Re-visit your goals and think if they reflect your true desires:

_____
_____
_____
_____
_____
_____
_____
_____
_____
_____
_____
_____
_____
_____

Woosah! Take a breather

CHAPTER 7: IT'S OKAY TO CHANGE YOUR MIND

As you grow, so will your ideals

Now that you have taken the time to reflect on what your true desires are we want to remind you that it is ok to do something different! No matter how old you are or how deep into the career you are. If you realize that you are not living or working within your passion it is perfectly okay to change your mind. Sometimes we feel "it's too late" to pick a new career or start that business. Truth be told, it's never too late to pursue true happiness! If we give ourselves permission to pursue happiness, we can be on our way to making our dreams a reality.

On your journey to self-actualization (Maslow's term for achieving one's full potential) the goals you feel you need to accomplish may change. Life and maturity have a funny way of changing our priorities for us. It's us to us to listen to our hearts and allow our brain to follow. The heart can fuel our passion, but our brain is what allows us to execute and finish what we start.

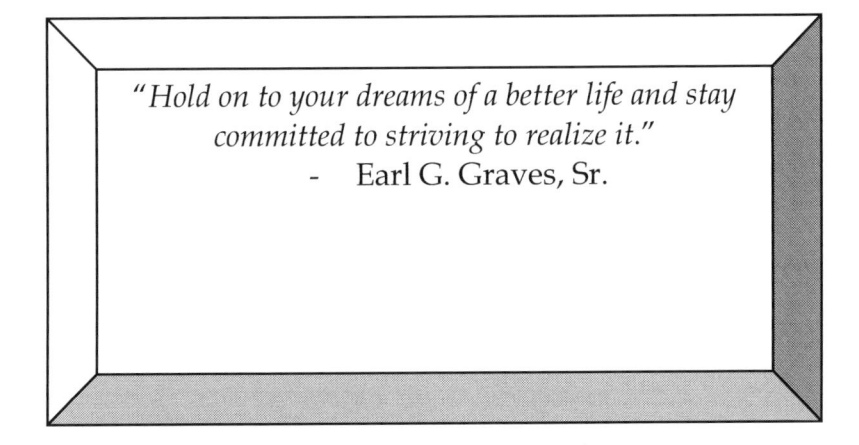

> *"Hold on to your dreams of a better life and stay committed to striving to realize it."*
> - Earl G. Graves, Sr.

Maslow's Hierarchy of Needs

Self-Actualization
Pursue talent, creativity, fulfillment

Self-Esteem
Achievement, Mastery, Recognition

Belonging
Friends, Family, Community

Safety
Security, Shelter

Physiological
Food, Water, Warmth

Please use the following lines to listen to your heart and jot down the things you are passionate about:

It's not failure!

Let's turn our attention to the ugly truth that we sometimes don't want to talk about, failure. Unfortunately, failure is a part of life and we all will experience it at some point in life. The real test is how we bounce back after we have failed. It is completely up to us to take that failure and instead of getting discouraged and down on ourselves we learn from it. In most cases there is always something to learn from a failure we just have to take the time to change our perception from "I should've known this wouldn't work out for me" to "This is a minor setback, but I can still make this happen!"

The small yet very impactful change of perception in the previously mentioned phrases can be the difference between you throwing in the towel or pushing forward and continuing the fight. Also, we must keep in mind that the rough journey makes the reward even sweeter. If your goal is worth having, then it's worth working for. So, stay strong and follow your heart.

Use the lines below to reflect on a time that you have tried something and failed at it. What did you learn from that particular failure?

It's okay to start over – better late than never.

Often times we view starting over as a negative thing. We see it in a negative light because we feel like we are throwing away all that we have done. In all actuality we are taking from the experience we've gained and now finally using it to fuel our passion. Everything happens for a reason, so when the opportunity presents itself to allow you to start over and do what you love don't let that opportunity pass you by.

It's okay to start over – better late than never.

Often times we view starting over as a negative thing. We see it in a negative light because we feel like we are throwing away all that we have done. In all actuality we are taking from the experience we've gained and now finally using it to fuel our passion. Everything happens for a reason, so when the opportunity presents itself to allow you to start over and do what you love don't let that opportunity pass you by.

Look at starting over as a chance to hit the reset button. While hitting the reset button you get to create the life you want knowing what you know now. Most people have said or heard the age-old phrase "If I knew then what I know now." It's time for us to all view starting over as getting a chance to incorporate the information you now know into your life so you can live up to your full potential and find true happiness.

> "There's a difference between giving up and starting over" - Unknown

Use the thought bubbles to write notes you feel your younger self would benefit from.

CHAPTER 8: POSITIVE VIBES – MINDFULNESS TECHNIQUES

Have positive thoughts

Positive thinking means that you approach situations in a more positive and productive way. It has many benefits.

- ➢ Lower rate of depression
- ➢ Increased coping skills
- ➢ Enhanced life span
- ➢ Better psychological and physical well-being

Positive thinking can start with positive self-talk (the unspoken thoughts that run through your mind). So, it is important that we identify negative self-talk so that we can check it when it happens.

Identifying negative thinking:

- ➢ **Filtering.** You magnify the negative aspects of a situation and filter out all the positive ones. For example, you had a great day at work. You completed your tasks ahead of time and were complimented for doing a speedy and thorough job. That evening, you focus only on your plan to do even more tasks and forget about the compliments you received.
- ➢ **Personalizing.** When something bad occurs, you automatically blame yourself. For example, you hear that an evening out with friends is canceled, and you assume that the change in plans is because no one wanted to be around you.
- ➢ **Catastrophizing.** You automatically anticipate the worst. The drive-through coffee shop gets your order wrong, and you automatically think that the rest of your day will be a disaster.
- ➢ **Polarizing.** You see things only as either good or bad. There is no middle ground. You feel that you must be perfect or you're a total failure.

Focusing on positive thinking

- **Identify areas to change.** If you want to become more optimistic and engage in more positive thinking, first identify areas of your life that you usually think negatively about, whether it's work, your daily commute, or a relationship. You can start small by focusing on one area to approach in a more positive way.

- **Check yourself.** Periodically during the day, stop and evaluate what you're thinking. If you find that your thoughts are mainly negative, try to find a way to put a positive spin on them.

- **Be open to humor.** Give yourself permission to smile or laugh, especially during difficult times. Seek humor in everyday happenings. When you can laugh at life, you feel less stressed.

- **Follow a healthy lifestyle.** Aim to exercise for about 30 minutes on most days of the week. You can also break it up into 10-minute chunks of time during the day. Exercise can positively affect mood and reduce stress. Follow a healthy diet to fuel your mind and body. And learn techniques to manage stress.

- **Surround yourself with positive people.** Make sure those in your life are positive, supportive people you can depend on to give helpful advice and feedback. Negative people may increase your stress level and make you doubt your ability to manage stress in healthy ways.

- **Practice positive self-talk.** Start by following one simple rule: Don't say anything to yourself that you wouldn't say to anyone else. Be gentle and encouraging with yourself. If a negative thought enters your mind, evaluate it rationally and respond with affirmations of what is good about you. Think about things you're thankful for in your life.

www.mayoclinic.org

Putting positive thinking into practice

Negative self-talk	Positive thinking
I've never done it before.	It's an opportunity to learn something new.
It's too complicated.	I'll tackle it from a different angle.
I don't have the resources.	Necessity is the mother of invention.
I'm too lazy to get this done.	I wasn't able to fit it into my schedule, but I can re-examine some priorities.
There's no way it will work.	I can try to make it work.
It's too radical a change.	Let's take a chance.

Use the lines below to reflect on times you let negative self-talk influence your decisions

S-O-S

Negative Self-Talk Stopping Technique

S-top: Mentally tell yourself "STOP!" to give you the opportunity to address the thought and interrupt the cycle.

O-bserve: Observe what you are saying to yourself and how it is making you feel.

S-hift: Shift your cognitive, emotional, or behavioral response by using positive coping skills and techniques

Think of ways that it can work

So, you have goals that you want to reach: note the obstacles that may hinder your goals and work a plan to overcome them.

> "If the plan doesn't work, change the plan, not the goal."
> - Unknown

Use these bubbles to jot down the things that you want for your life

Look for the silver lining

Silver linings are the good aspects of challenging situations. Finding the silver lining in stressful situations is a great coping tool.

> "Keep your face to the sunshine and you cannot see a shadow." - Helen Keller

Here are some tips on finding the silver lining:

- Be optimistic
- Be grateful
- Practice compassion
- Do service work
- Find things to look forward to
- Find good role models
- Know your triggers
- Use positive mantras
- Practice forgiveness
- Do things that bring you joy
- Be flexible

www.positivepsychology.com

Woosah! Take a breather

CHAPTER 9: CONSIDER ALTERNATIVES

Exploring what you can gain instead of dwelling on what you have lost.

All too often in life we are faced with negative situations and hard times. Sometimes we start to feel like "if it ain't one thing, it's another." If you've had this feeling or even said this phrase don't worry because you are not alone! This is a common feeling that most people have and sometimes it can be challenging to overcome. This chapter will help you take some of the common unfortunate situations we face, shift your mindset, and help you put and positive spin on them. Like we mentioned earlier this is called Cognitive Reframing. Once you have successfully shifted your mindset to be more positive, then you can begin using some positive self-talk to keep yourself motivated and hopeful. Keeping hope alive and staying motivated is half the battle to accomplishing your goals and having a sense of peace in a world that thrives off negativity.

> "Every negative thought is a down payment on your failure. Every positive thought is an investment on your future" - Unknown

Life Event	Negative Response (dwelling on what you lost)	Positive Response (Looking at what you can gain)
Being laid off from your job.	What am I going to do? I need this job; I live check to check!	This gives me a chance to apply for jobs that I am qualified for that also align with my passion.
Divorce/Romantic Relationship ending badly	I hate him/her, and I want them to hurt like I hurt. It must be something I did. I'm going to grow old and alone.	Everything happens for a reason. I gave the relationship my all and the next person will appreciate my efforts.
Did poorly on a big test. (SAT, GRE, etc.)	Everything I touch goes bad. I'm stupid. Who am I to think I can get a good score?	I messed up this time, but I am going to come back strong next time. I got this!

"If you realized how powerful your thoughts are, you would never think a negative thought again." - Unknown

Often, it is easy to fall into the trap of those negative responses listed above. When we feel or notice ourselves developing that negative tone or outlook, we must be mindful of that and make a conscious effort to shift into a positive space. To do that sometimes we need to practice some mindfulness techniques.

Mindfulness Techniques you can try:

- Taking time to meditate. (YouTube has some great guided meditations that are free)
- Yoga
- Listen to music that uplifts you (Create a Positivity Playlist with songs that make you happy and make you want to sing and dance)
- The 5 Senses Grounding Exercise (Sit comfortably in a quiet room and look for 5 things you can see that are the same color, 4 things you can touch that are comforting, 3 things you can hear, 2 things you can smell, and 1 thing you can taste. This exercise aims to help us relax and live in the present moment)
- Going for a walk or bike ride outside.
- Saying a positive mantra to yourself or using positive self-talk while looking in the mirror. (Think of a positive saying/mantra that could help you in your time of need)
- Use a weighted blanket or pillow. The weight of the blanket or pillow can help ground you and they help some people relax.
- Have a hobby. Especially one that allows your brain to be free from stress and turns on your creativity. (Cooking, Art, Puzzles, etc.)
- Last but not least Journaling! …….clearly, you're already hip to journaling and its benefits.

There are obviously way more mindfulness options out there, but we just wanted to give you a few to get you started. Below we want you to think of some things you could do to relax and jot them down below.

Now that you have thought about things you can do to relax and help you live in the present moment lets revisit how we respond to those unexpected life events.

Use the chart below to think of an unexpected life event that happened to you, how you handled it, and what you feel you would do differently if you were faced with this situation again.

Life Event	How did you handle it?/How did you feel when it happened?	How could you have handled it differently?/What could have been a positive view of the situation?

> *Get yourself grounded and you can navigate even the stormiest roads in peace.*
> — Steve Goodier

Just in case you have gotten to this point and are wondering "what does grounding even mean?" Grounding, when referring to mindfulness, is the ability to return to the present moment with sustained attention. By returning to the present moment, you have regulated your emotions and remained in control rather than letting your emotions get the best of you. We all have the power to stay in control and regulate our emotions. Having emotions is a great thing but when they take control, we sometime act on impulse rather than doing what is best. We encourage you to incorporate some mindfulness techniques and grounding exercises into your self-care routine. In order to take care of others you must take care of yourself first! Now is the time to make yourself and your mental health a priority.

Woosah! Take a breather

CHAPTER 10: BUCKET LIST

A bucket list is a number of experiences or achievements that a person would like to accomplish during their lifetime.

Creating a bucket list can help you tap into the creative part of yourself, the part of you that dreams bigger and makes life worthwhile.

> "The goal is to die with memories, not dreams." - Unknown

> "The biggest adventure you can take is to live the life of your dreams." – Oprah Winfrey

Bucket List Ideas:

- Go on a wildlife safari
- Go on a week-long cruise
- Run a marathon
- Road-trip across the entire United States
- Visit the Grand Canyon
- Swim the major oceans
- Visit the 7 wonders of the world
- Start your own business
- Become a mentor
- Master a new skill
- Take a cooking class
- Ride a mechanical bull
- Donate to charity
- Learn a new language
- Learn to play an instrument
- Adopt a rescue animal
- Go to a Broadway show
- Ride horses on the beach
- Go skinny dipping
- Conquer a fear
- Make a viral video
- Go on an African safari
- Paint a piece of art for your home
- Write a book
- Learn to play chess
- Take a dance class
- Take a ride on a hot air balloon

Use the following pages to plan your bucket list:

SOCIAL MEDIA

Below is a list of social media (Instagram) handles you may enjoy:

- @ gyst_pub
- @ iam.mantra
- @ soyouwanttotalkabout
- @ resilientchildtherapy
- @ relatingtoyou_
- @ mybrownbox
- @ dedicationcounseling
- @ mahoganymhc
- @ balanceandbloomco
- @ authenticconnectionsts
- @ haarppp.llc

- @ citadelcounselingservices

- @ minds_in_motion_therapy

- @ zeppwellness

- @ talkspace

- @ blackmentalwellness

- @ marriagerecoverycenter

- @ ayana_therapy

- @ melaninandmentalhealth

- @ thebehappyproject

- @ pathway2success1

- @ therapyforblackgirls

- @ therapyforblkmen

- @ selfcareisforeveryone

- @ thegoodquote

- @ realdepressionproject

- @ mentalhealthamerica

- @ lighthouse._therapy

REFERENCES & RESOURCES

www.christinebradstreet.com

www.healthline.com

www.mayoclinic.org

www.positivepsychology.com

www.psychologytoday.com

www.quotesgram.com

www.thriveglobal.com

www.verwellmind.com

THANK YOU!

We are so grateful of your choice to go on this journal journey!

Please check us out:

Social Media Handles:
Instagram:
Gyst_pub
Wise_answers

Facebook:
GYST Publications